362.29   Smith, Sandra Lee
SMI
          Peyote and magic
          mushrooms

                                        21569

$15.95

DATE			

PEYOTE AND MAGIC MUSHROOMS

Hallucinogens can distort your perception of reality.

THE DRUG ABUSE PREVENTION LIBRARY

PEYOTE AND MAGIC MUSHROOMS

Sandra Lee Smith

THE ROSEN PUBLISHING GROUP, INC.
NEW YORK

Dedicated to my husband, Ed, and the memory of our year in Latin America.

The people pictured in this book are only models; they in no way practice or endorse the activities illustrated. Captions serve only to explain the subjects of photographs and do not in any way imply a connection between the real-life models and the staged situations shown.

Published in 1995 by The Rosen Publishing Group, Inc.
29 East 21st Street, New York, NY 10010

First Edition

Library of Congress Cataloging-in-Publication Data
Smith, Sandra Lee.
  Peyote and magic mushrooms / Sandra Lee Smith.
    p.   cm. — (The Drug abuse prevention library)
  Includes bibliographical references and index.
  ISBN 0-8239-1700-2
  1. Hallucinogenic plants—Juvenile literature.
2. Peyote—Juvenile literature. 3. Mushrooms,
Hallucinogenic—Juvenile literature. 4. Drug abuse—
Prevention—Juvenile literature. [1. Peyote.
2. Mushrooms, Hallucinogenic. 3. Drugs. 4. Drug
abuse.] I. Title. II. Series.
HV5822.H25S64   1994
  362.29′4—dc20   94-2268
                                                        CIP
                                                         AC

Manufactured in the United States of America

Contents

Introduction

"*T*his is great!" Sean hollered as the wind whipped past his face. "We're free."

"Really free," Danny agreed as he stretched his arms out the window of Sean's 4 × 4 Mazda Navajo. "I still can't believe our folks let us come West."

"The wide open spaces." Sean gestured toward the prairie stretching out on all sides.

"Can you believe this? I mean, we read about the open spaces in Montana, but until you see it for real . . ." Danny shook his head in amazement.

"I can hardly wait to get to the Rockies. I hear they're awesome."

"My cousin went to Yellowstone last

Teens who smoke and drink are often tempted to try stronger drugs like peyote or magic mushrooms.

8 | year and saw all kinds of wild animals."

"Animals!" Sean laughed. "The only animals I want to see are some female party animals."

Danny laughed. "My cousin said there were lots of those too."

"All right!"

Music blared from the rear speakers. Sean and Danny sang along and snapped their fingers to the beat as it pulsated throughout the cab. Danny rolled a joint and lit up. The sweet-smelling smoke of the marijuana curled around them.

"You wanna know what I heard?" Sean lowered the volume when the song ended. Without waiting for an answer, he continued. "My brother, you know, the one who's away at college?"

Danny nodded.

"He told me that the Indians out here eat peyote and get really high."

Danny straightened, his attention fully on Sean. "Isn't that a cactus plant?"

"Sure is," Sean agreed, "and it's like taking PCP."

"That's heavy stuff. Isn't it what Cassie blew her mind on last spring?"

"Yeah. She got a bad deal. This stuff's safe, though. It's a natural plant, so you don't get screwed by an overdose."

"I wonder how we can get some? Does it grow out here?" Danny glanced out at the fields of grass waving in the breeze.

"Naw. I think it comes from Mexico."

"How do the Indians get it then?" Danny asked.

"They're allowed to have it. Something about their religion."

Danny put out the joint. His favorite song came on, and he turned up the volume. Ahead, a pickup truck blocked the road. Sean braked the Navajo and stopped beside it.

"Need any help?" Sean hollered when he saw pieces of rubber on the road.

A tall, dark youth stood and approached their truck. "My tire blew." He pointed to the smashed rim. "I don't have a spare."

"Is there a town nearby?" Sean asked. "We can give you a lift."

"No," the youth answered, his long braid of black hair swinging as he shook his head.

"You an Indian?" Danny blurted out.

"Lakota," he said easily. "My name's Charley Blue Eyes. My people live here." He gestured toward the plains. "We're having a powwow and I'm late. I could use a lift."

Spanish explorers noted that the Aztecs, an ancient people who once lived near what is now Mexico City, often used hallucinogenic mushrooms. These are Aztec ruins.

Without hesitating, Sean stepped out of the cab and made room behind his seat. "Hop in. We'll get you there."

Sean hadn't driven far when Charley Blue Eyes directed him to turn off. The dirt road was rutted and narrow, making Sean glad he had four-wheel drive.

After an hour of rough travel, they entered a wide valley with a river running through it. To Sean and Danny's amazement, hundred of vehicles were parked in the open field. Several hundred people were camped along the river: some in campers, others in trailers, tents, and—to their astonishment— tepees.

Charley Blue Eyes took them around, explaining who everyone was and where they were from. "There are tribes from all over the U.S. here."

"What are they all doing?" Sean asked.

"It's a powwow. Everybody comes together to trade and visit. We also hold competitive dance competitions. It's great."

"Do you eat peyote?" Danny asked.

Suddenly Charley Blue Eyes grew silent. Sean glanced up to see three men standing beside them.

"We are grateful to you for helping my son," the older man spoke. "But now you must leave."

"But . . . ," Sean began.

Charley Blue Eyes cut him off. "Follow me. I'll show you the way."

"Your dad seemed upset," Danny commented.

"You should not have mentioned the peyote," Charley Blue Eyes explained. "My father takes such things seriously. He does not want anyone being disrespectful to his way of life. Not here, anyway, among his people."

12 | Sean tried to apologize, but Charley Blue Eyes seemed not to hear. With a stony expression, he showed them how to find their way back to the highway.

"Be thankful he didn't have you arrested. The fact that you helped me out saved your hides."

"But we didn't do anything wrong," Sean protested.

"You're in the Lakota Nation now. We have our own laws here."

Twenty-eight states have laws either supporting or denying Native Americans' use of peyote as a part of their religious ceremonies. The Native American Church has petitioned the Supreme Court to create a uniform federal standard for peyote use by members of the church and Native Americans. That legislation is pending.

In the past, the native peoples of the Americas used many drugs from plants that grew in various regions. If the plants did not grow locally, they were obtained in trade for use in ceremonies and for medicines. One of the most common plants, which is still used by some Native Americans, is peyote.

Another common plant used by Native Americans of Canada and Latin America

In the 1950s, many politicians were insensitive to the rights of Native Americans. Here Dr. Clarence Salsbury shows three peyote cacti at a press conference.

14 | are magic mushrooms. These have much the same effect as peyote and are also used for medicinal and spiritual purposes.

A few tribes that live in isolated regions of the mountains avoided the white man's culture and still today live much as they did hundreds of years ago. It is from these tribes that scientists have gained most of their current knowledge about peyote and magic mushrooms.

Similar but Different

The two plants look very different when growing, but they are very much alike when dried for use. They both look shriveled and black. They also have the same effect on the human body. Peyote and magic mushrooms cause an altered state of mind. They contain different chemicals, but some of the chemicals in both are hallucinogenic. This means that they cause a person's mind to hallucinate, to see and hear things that are not there. The reaction is similar to that of LSD and PCP, which are other mind-altering drugs.

Peyote comes from the button-shaped fruit of a small cactus that grows in southern Texas and parts of Central Mexico. *Psilocybe* mushrooms are used by a few tribes in the mountains of southern

Mexico. However, other kinds of magic mushrooms grow in many parts of North, South, and Central America.

The use of peyote and mushrooms in religious ceremonies became forbidden as the native American cultures were destroyed by European Christians. With recent pressure in society to allow for cultural diversity, the use of the plants has again become more widespread. The present concern is the widespread use and misuse by teens and adults. They find peyote and mushrooms without knowing which ones may be poisonous. They rush into eating the plant without proper mental preparation. This is extremely dangerous. Not only do they endanger themselves physically, but they are breaking the law.

It must be understood that these drugs are illegal substances and are dangerous to use. It is against the law to use peyote or magic mushrooms in Canada, the United States, and in Mexico and the rest of Latin America. Use of these drugs can result in stiff prison sentences.

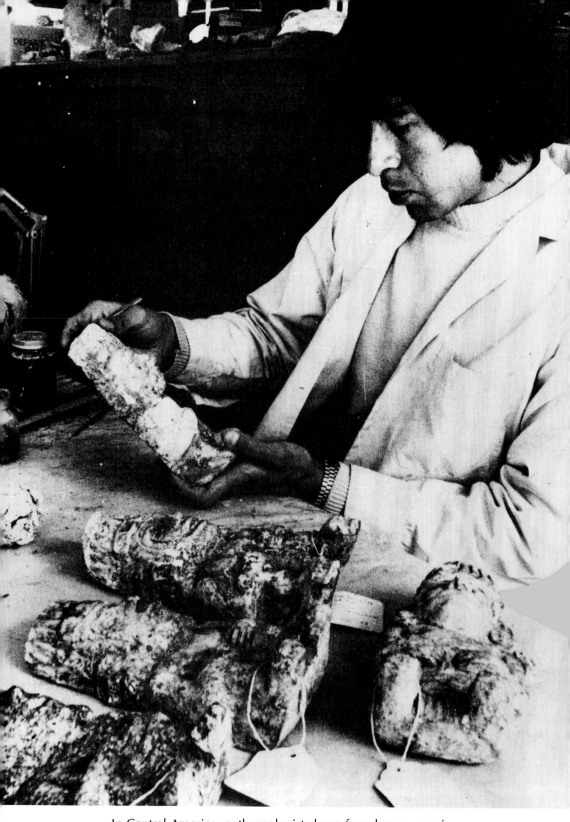

In Central America, anthropologists have found many carvings
of gods depicted as mushrooms.

CHAPTER 1

Historical Use of Peyote and Mushrooms

Since prehistoric times, peyote and mushrooms have been used in religious ceremonies in efforts to contact the gods or the spirit world. Tribes of people have used the plants for spiritual revelations and for healing purposes. Anthropologists claim that use of hallucinogenic plants has been traced to the Bronze Age (about 3000 BC). They believe that actual use goes back to the Mesolithic period of about 9000 BC.

The plants were also used by ancient peoples to numb the senses to the pain of illness or injury. When eaten daily, they helped to ease hunger or discontent.

In some cases only the shaman or

18 medicine man used the drugs. In other cases all members of the community ate the plants.

The most common plant used for mind-altering purposes is the mushroom. Of over 50,000 known species, 2 percent are known to be hallucinogenic. These mushrooms fall into two types: fly agaric (*Amanita muscaria*) and *Psilocybe mexicana*. Generally, fly agaric is found in the Northern Hemisphere and Psilocybe in the equatorial zones of the Americas.

Early records show use of the mushroom by ancient Hindus. Anthropologists believe it is referred to in the *Rig Veda*, an ancient Sanskrit epic. They have also found evidence of widespread use in pre-Christian Europe. Use today by native tribes in Siberia hint at the ways the fly agaric mushroom was used in Europe.

Fly Agaric

Many folk tales and old sayings refer to mushrooms, usually mentioning madness or crazy behavior. The fly agaric mushroom of Europe and Siberia gets its name because the red-capped mushrooms attract flies and yet are poisonous to them. For centuries people have soaked these

Atlantic
Ocean

Tropic of Cancer

Equator

Pacific
Ocean

Tropic of Capricorn

**The area in which psylocibe
mushrooms are found**

☐ Mushrooms

mushrooms in milk and then placed
the liquid around their homes to kill
flies.

With the advent of Christianity to
Europe, names of ancient gods were
transformed into Satan and his evil
demons. Flies were associated with the
devil. *Beelzebub,* an ancient Hebrew
word for "Lord of flies," is a name for
Satan.

In spite of the negative effects of fly
agaric mushrooms, people continued to
eat them in efforts to contact the spirit
world. Even today, indigenous tribes in
far Siberia regularly eat them.

20 | *A Secondhand High*

When the mushrooms are scarce, these people drink their own urine or the urine of others who have eaten the mushrooms, seeking the high from the alkaloids in the mushrooms. These alkaloids do not break down when they pass through a human body. Some natives claim to have stayed high up to a week after eating mushrooms once. They drink their urine over and over again to get full use of the hallucinogenic chemicals they have consumed.[1]

Some tribes migrated from Europe to Siberia and from there to the Americas. It is believed that the tradition of eating hallucinogenic mushrooms went with them. The mushrooms have been found growing in the Pacific Northwest and in parts of Canada. The Ojibwa and Chippewa of the Great Lakes region in Canada have been known to use fly agaric in their healing ceremonies.[2]

Most mushroom use in the Americas was by the tribes of Mexico, Central America, and South America. The mush-

---

[1] Peter T. Furst, PhD, *Mushrooms, Psychedelic Fungi* (New York: Chelsea House Publishers), 1992

[2] Ibid.

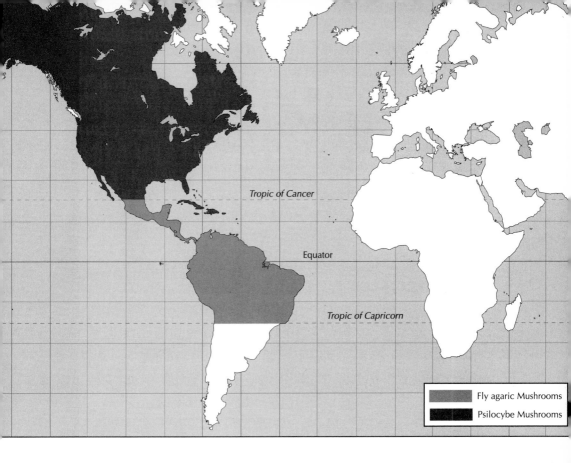

Tropic of Cancer

Equator

Tropic of Capricorn

Fly agaric Mushrooms

Psilocybe Mushrooms

rooms they used, however, were not fly agaric. The mushrooms growing in these regions are quite different.

Psilocybe

The mushrooms here that contain the hallucinogenic psilocybin or psilocin are those of the genus *Psilocybe mexicana*. These are a higher order of the mushroom family and grow in hot and humid climates. They are often found growing out of animal feces, which helps in identifying them.

Psilocybe mushrooms are shown in clay

22 | sculptures, stone carvings, and figurines of the ancient pre-Columbian peoples. There are many figures of people with mushroom caps for heads or growing out of their ears or necks. Often these mushroom figures represent the shamans or priests of the culture.

It is believed that mushrooms were used by the Aztecs in sacrificing humans. Figures show women grinding the mushrooms into powder in mortar and pestle. Other carvings show the powder being thrown into the faces of the victims before their heads are cut off.

Arrival of the Spaniards

When the Spanish came to the Americas they noted many instances of mushroom use by the Aztecs. Because the user behaves so oddly, mushroom eaters were considered crazy or mad. The fact that the mushrooms were used in human sacrifice led the Spanish to believe they were indeed a substance of Satan.

The rite of sacrifice was shocking to the Catholic priests who came with the Spaniards to the Americas. When the Spaniards gained political control, they were urged by the priests to forbid human sacrifice as well as the use of drugs.

In the process of passing these laws, the Spanish destroyed most written records of the use of the plants. The conquest of the Americas was closely followed by the Inquisition, a Catholic tribunal to investigate heresy. The mushroom and peyote rites were ruled to be of the devil and were banned. Much of the use of peyote and mushrooms died out when the Spanish destroyed the Aztec culture and people.

Mushroom Gods

The Aztecs had used the mushrooms extensively. The Mayans, a pre-Columbian culture that was centered in Guatemala and the Yucatan Peninsula, knew about the hallucinogenic mushrooms. They associated them with the supernatural forces that controlled weather. In fact, one of the mushrooms is named *Kakulja,* which means lightning bolt.

In Central America, anthropologists have found many carvings of gods depicted as mushrooms. The images show that these peoples, like the mushroom eaters in Europe and Siberia, connect their experiences to the spirit world. The Spanish conquerors believed that a mushroom cult may have been in existence at

24 | the time. The mushroom god-like figures lead anthropologists to agree.

Peyote

The mushroom was not the only plant to have hallucinogenic properties. The Native Americans knew about datura, a plant having hallucinogenic properties, and tobacco as well. They also used peyote in northern Mexico.

Peyote was used by the peoples of Mexico for centuries. Its use is recorded in ancient writings of the Aztecs. Pictographs of the plant exist. Stone figures and statues show figures dancing around the plants or wearing the button flowers on their bodies.

The Huichol Indians of northern Mexico provide us with the best example of how the plant was used, since they use it in much the same way today.

Peyote is believed by these people to be a god. They contact the god to help them identify illnesses. Most Native Americans believed—and some still do believe—that sickness and death are caused by spiritual forces working within the body. It was important, therefore, to confront the spirits that were causing an illness.

The shaman contacted the spirit world

with the help of hallucinogenic plants and asked the peyote god to intervene. Believing that he was actually in the spirit world, the shaman would battle the evil spirits that were causing the harm.[3]

In the same way, the shaman was believed to be able to overcome curses and to protect his people from witchcraft invoked by enemies. This belief in evil spirits, and the terrifying hallucinations that can occur with use of peyote, were what convinced the Spaniards that peyote was an agent of Satan.

Destruction of Knowledge

Juan de Zumanaga, the first archbishop of Mexico, searched out all mention of mind-altering drugs, including peyote and psychedelic mushrooms, and had records of their use destroyed. In the process they destroyed records of all plants used for medicinal purposes. This act they later regretted, realizing that they had destroyed good along with what they thought was evil.

In the 17th century, Spanish scholars tried to recover what evidence they could

[3] Edward F. Anderson, *The Divine Cactus* (Tucson, University of Arizona Press), 1985.

26 about the use of plants for medicinal purposes. They found that peyote and mushrooms were used for healing, but because of the plants' association with the spirit world, the scientists maintained they were evil and their use was discontinued.

Since the Inquisition was in session at the same time period, use of hallucinogenic plants was associated with the devil. In fact, one of the questions the priests asked the native people was, "Have you eaten peyote?" They also asked, "Hast thou loved any created thing, adoring it, looking upon it as God and worshiping it?" Many answered that they believed in the sacred herb, the *peyotl*.[4]

From the known history of both peyote and the psychedelic mushrooms, we can see that these plants were always connected to the culture's views of the spirit world. To some they were evil spirits. To others they were helpful gods that told fortunes and healed sickness. The use of the hallucinogens has historically been connected with man's search for the divine.

---

[4] Ibid.

Many people in the 1960s traveled West in search of mushrooms and peyote as a part of a new generation's quest for a new way of living.

CHAPTER 2

Modern Use of Psychedelic Plants

*T*he European explorers destroyed most aspects of Native American culture and lifestyle. In the process they focused especially on rooting out traditions that used peyote, mushrooms, and other mind-altering plants on the grounds that they were tricks of the devil. Only isolated Native American tribes were still practicing the ancient traditions and rites. These peoples lived in mountainous areas that were hard to reach until recent times.

In the late 19th and early 20th centuries anthropologists discovered these tribes and began to study them. They focused much of their research on the use of plants in religious ceremonies. Publica-

tion of this research brought wide attention to these tribes and especially to their
use of peyote and *Psilocybe* mushrooms.

The American hippies in the 1960s
and the counterculture movement of
the early '70s readily picked up on the
research and flocked to Mexico and Latin
America in search of the "divine high."
This steady stream of travelers nearly
destroyed the isolated native cultures.

Since the effects of the mushrooms
and peyote were so similar to those of
LSD, the plants aroused interest as hallucinogens. It was known that LSD was
extremely dangerous. Peyote and mushrooms were mistakenly thought to be
safer because they were natural sources of
the chemicals and alkaloids. This popular-
ity of the plants increased the demand for
them in the United States and Canada.

Coming Together of Tribes

At the same time, Native American tribes
in the United States were beginning to
unite as a people. This brought their
many different cultures together, and they
began sharing rites and ceremonies. The
peyote rite was taught to the tribes by
those who had been in Texas and learned
about the plant's use there. In efforts to

30 bring Western beliefs around to the Indian way of thinking, many tribes adopted the use of peyote in religious ceremonies. It became especially popular in healing rites.

The Native American Church soon adopted peyote as part of their ritual. They believed in Christianity, but felt that many teachings of the Bible were meant only for the white man because it was he who had crucified Christ. Since the Indian was not part of that sin, they believed they could talk to God through the peyote god, whom they met when they ate the peyote during their sacred ceremonies.[1]

The members of the Native American Church talked to the peyote god and asked him what evil spirits were causing someone to be ill. They also asked him about decisions to make for their future. The peyote god helped them fight off evil spirits.

Ban on Peyote
When the U.S. Congress passed the Comprehensive Abuse Prevention and

---

[1] Edward F. Anderson, *Peyote, the Divine Cactus* (Tucson: University of Arizona Press), 1985.

Control Act of 1970, many things happened to change the use of peyote and psychedelic mushrooms. The Native American Church petitioned a court for the legal right to use peyote in their rites. They based their claim on the right to religious freedom guaranteed in the U.S. Constitution. The battle, however, made the public aware of the use of peyote by the church, even though the right to use peyote was later canceled.

Teens began to infringe on the privacy of the tribes by seeking Indian "friends" who would take them to their church for a peyote high. This was very offensive to people who took their religion and ceremonies seriously.

In Mexico, Americans and Europeans did the same thing, seeking out isolated tribes to buy peyote and mushrooms. This brought the modern world into the native cultures and is likely to destroy them.

Use of hallucinogenic plants by these Mexican tribes involves extensive ceremony, tradition, and careful selection and preparation of the plants. The people who eat the plants also need to be mentally prepared so that they will not have a bad experience. Extreme care is taken in

32 choosing the plants, as there are poisonous varieties of peyote and mushrooms.

Dangers of Arrest
The cooperation between the United States and Mexico in the drug war has prompted the Mexican government to make peyote and *Psilocybe* mushrooms illegal. Consequently many young people are being arrested. This is extremely dangerous, because in foreign countries Americans have no rights as they do in the United States and Canada, where you are innocent until proven guilty. In Mexico one is guilty until proven innocent. Many teens are still suffering in Mexican prisons.

In U.S. prisons, inmates are fed and clothed and have television, libraries, and games for entertainment. In Mexico prisoners must provide their own clothing, food, and bedding. There are no games, no television, and often no heat or air conditioning. Prisoners have to work and buy their food with their own money.

The white slave trade is another danger teens face in Mexico, especially along the border. Drug dealers are sometimes connected with slave traders. Often teens who contact these dealers end up in the

Some American teens suspected of drug use in Mexico
have simply disappeared.

34 | slave trade. Blond females are favorites of the slave traders because they can easily be sold for prostitution.

Not only are prison conditions unhealthy and miserable, but prisoners are often abused. Many American teens have been beaten by *Federales*, or Mexican federal officers, before being arrested. Often, *Federales* beat teens simply on suspicion and ask questions later.

Many teens suspected of drug use in Mexico have simply disappeared. American families have spent years and thousands of dollars searching for family members who have been suspected of drug use and disappeared. Many gruesome stories circulate, such as teens being flown over the Pacific and dumped out of the plane.

Street Dealers

Most teens do not travel to an Indian reservation nor to Mexico to obtain peyote or mushrooms. They resort to drug dealers on the streets. Since it is obviously an illegal operation, the sale of these drugs is unregulated. This means there is no sure way to know that what you are buying is peyote or magic mushrooms.

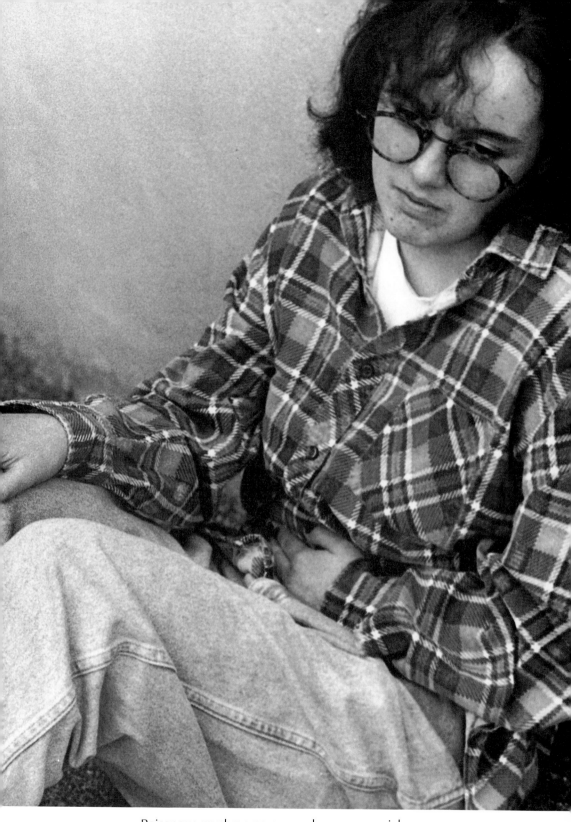

Poisonous mushrooms can make you very sick.

36   Fresh mushrooms and peyote are easily identified, but they last only a few days. To transport them to cities and dealers, they are frozen and placed in plastic bags. This process turns them black and misshapen. Then you can't tell the difference between a peyote button and a mushroom.

Turning Good Mushrooms Bad

Ordinary store varieties of mushrooms that are frozen look exactly like frozen *Psilocybe*. Dealers sometimes buy mushrooms at the grocery store and "lace" them, or insert PCP or LSD into them with a hypodermic needle. People who eat these mushrooms have the same hallucinations and believe they have real *Psilocybe* or peyote. No one can be sure how much LSD or PCP has been injected into these mushrooms. LSD and PCP are also known to be very dangerous drugs.

    Another development in recent years is that people are realizing that fly agaric mushrooms similar to those found in Europe and Siberia are common in some forested areas of the United States and Canada. It takes an expert, however, to tell the difference between the fly agaric and the poisonous varieties. Many red-capped mushrooms look like fly agaric but are extremely poisonous.

Not only do people pick them for their own use, but many are picked and sold to street dealers. Neither the people picking the mushrooms nor the dealers know the difference between fly agaric and the poisonous plants. Thus the poisonous plants are sold to unsuspecting victims.

Many people have purchased bad mushrooms from dealers. Others have sought out the mushrooms themselves and have ended up with a poisonous variety instead of a hallucinogenic type. Some of these people have become very sick or died.

Natural vs. Dangerous

Peyote and *Psilocybe* mushrooms have been defined as narcotics and as two of the most dangerous drugs on the market today. The fact that they are "natural" plants does not mean they are not potentially harmful. Just because they haven't been proved addictive does not mean they won't damage your body. Anytime you alter the chemical balance of your body, you are exposing yourself to harm.

Many people have gone insane from bad trips on hallucinogenics. Many have

38 reported visions so terrifying that they have lost touch with reality. Some people claim to have seen hell. Others claim to have seen demons so horrifying that they have nightmares long after taking the drug. Seeing these things makes one extremely fearful and anxious. That is why users are often declared crazy or mad or insane.

Some users have experienced extreme pain as if a leg or an arm were being cut off. Some actually visualize body parts falling off of them. They see themselves so distorted and ugly that it frightens them terribly.

It is believed that the effect of the chemicals makes some people so frightened that they think they will die. Sometimes they actually do die. Hallucinogenic drugs act on the suggestible part of the brain until you actually believe what you are thinking about.

Psychedelic drugs are not something to experiment with. Altering your mind can result in permanent damage to the brain and the way it functions.

CHAPTER 3

What Is Really Happening?

*P*eyote and mushrooms contain different chemicals that produce the mind-altering effects. Peyote contains mescaline and other minor substances that cause hallucinations. Fly agaric mushrooms have chemicals called muscimol and ibotenic acid. The muscimol is the hallucinogen and the chemical that does not break down in the body. It is what allows for the additional highs the Siberians gain from drinking urine.

The mushrooms of Mexico and Central and South America contain a psychoactive alkaloid called psilocybin after the *Psilocybe* mushroom. Psilocybin and LSD are in the tryptamine chemical group. Mescaline is a member of the

40 | phenylethylamine group. Both of these groups are hallucinogenic agents.

Dosages of Hallucinogens

Even though the chemicals that cause hallucinations are different in these plants, they all produce the same experiences. Different dosages, however, are required to obtain the same reaction or high. One or two micrograms of LSD per kilogram of body weight will produce the same reaction as 5,000 to 10,000 micrograms of mescaline per kilogram of body weight. The average dose of psilocybin is 100 to 200 micrograms per kilogram of body weight.

The reactions to these average doses are very similar. Some of the basic effects on the body are:

1. Slight increase in blood pressure and pulse rate
2. Strong increase in knee reflex. High doses produce flailing of the legs and arms. (This is what makes people think users are mad or crazy.)
3. Dilated pupils
4. Strange gait and changes in posture

Using hallucinogens can upset your sense of balance.

5. Increase in motor activity, such as fidgeting
6. Immediate perspiring
7. Rapid breathing
8. For the first four hours, lowered body temperature, then high temperature
9. Rapid rise in blood sugar, causing dizziness
10. Decrease in blood potassium
11. Increase in need to urinate and defecate
12. Flushing of the skin, often accompanied by shivering and chills

42

13. Increased salivation
14. Sensations of hot and cold.

How the Brain Reacts

In the brain the alkaloids cause a general flattening of wavelengths and a blocking of the alpha rhythm when the user is visualizing. The drug binds the brain's normal screening process and therefore allows in large amounts of stimulus. That causes the mind to hallucinate or see things out of proportion.

For example, our eyes look at objects in the kitchen and tell the brain what they see. The brain then puts things in proportion to size. The table might be the same size as the stove top, and the brain transmits that information. If the screening process is not working, however, the brain might record the table as four times larger than the stove. You think it is, because your brain told you wrong.

Many people believe that they see a display of colors. They are really seeing the correct color, but the drug makes the brain report the colors as brighter or different than they really are. When we see a color, it activates a response in the brain that tells us what color we see. The drug however, activates those response centers so that we "see" colors even with our eyes closed. | *43*

A person who eats peyote or *Psilocybe* or fly agaric mushrooms has hallucinations. A hallucination is seeing things that are not really there.

Stages of Distortion

Most people who take peyote have simple visions, mainly flashes of light and color. Some people see familiar objects such as people or animals or places they know.

Mushroom eaters often experience a sense of strength and an increase in agility. In fact, some users claim they can perform feats of endurance or strength like running for hours or lifting extremely heavy objects.

The next stage of intoxication involves many more hallucinations as well as distortion in the size of objects. For example, a knife might appear so large that it has to be grasped with both hands. Or a stairway might look so steep that a person takes extra large steps to climb it.

Users often have a sense of not being connected to their body. Sometimes only parts seem connected, as if the hands and arms are floating free. This causes many users to hold their bodies or walk peculiarly. Often it is difficult to talk.

44 Because of these distortions of physical reality, and the extreme emotions that occur when taking the drugs, many users become extremely frightened during the experience. They can become so disoriented that they harm themselves or others. Sometimes they imagine a sense of pain so intense that they actually injure themselves trying to get away from the pain.

Power of Suggestion

A common claim is that these drugs heighten the sex drive. People who use peyote seldom have any interest in sex. However, since hallucinogens change the perceptions of events, they may think they have had a sexual experience when they actually have not. Some people claim to have had strong sexual desires, but these are very rare. The mind-set of people taking the drugs is usually not in a mode directed at sexual pursuits.

Most people who have studied the use of peyote and mushrooms believe that the chemicals move a person strongly by the power of suggestion. Usually, whatever the person is thinking about before becoming affected by the drug is what happens in the hallucinations or dreams. For example, if you are convinced that you will see and speak to gods, when you enter the advanced stages of intoxication that is what you see and do. The Native American tribes who use peyote or mushrooms go through long and detailed preparations. For days they take very careful steps to pick the right plants. Then they usually fast or eat only certain foods. Special music such as drums and chanting is used. The whole experience is so closely linked to their culture and belief system that it is too complicated to understand without years of study.

Many people believe that the reason users die from hallucinogenic mushrooms is that their minds are not properly prepared. The belief has been so ingrained that the mushrooms are poisonous that people who are unprepared may think they have been poisoned. As soon as the physical effects of rapid pulse and shortness of breath occur, they may become so afraid of dying that in their heightened state of fear they actually do die.

Allergic Reactions

Another real danger in eating any plant like peyote or mushrooms is the possibility of an allergic reaction. Allergies can cause a person to break out in a rash, be

46 short of breath, and become violently ill with convulsions or vomiting. Some allergic reactions result in death.

Some users who live through a bad experience never quite recover from it mentally nor emotionally. The trauma is so terrifying that a form of madness sets in. Some people have seen such horrible creatures in their hallucinations that they are fearful and nervous all the time. Another common occurrence is that the mind has been so shocked that the user has difficulty thinking straight and seems stupid and confused.

It is no accident that the ancient and common names for mushrooms are "crazy mushrooms," "mad mushrooms," and "fool's mushrooms." In some countries in Europe, instead of saying, "Have you gone out of your mind?" they ask, "Have you eaten crazy mushrooms?"

Mushrooms and peyote alter your state of mind. Therefore the setting, your experiences, and your emotions will greatly affect the hallucinations you have. The physical reaction to the chemicals also affects your reaction. It is far too dangerous to take chances with your health and your sanity. Sampling these dangerous drugs could result in a lifetime of regret.

CHAPTER 4

Where to Find Help

*S*ince peyote and mushrooms have not been found to be physically addictive, treatment centers are not really needed to break physical dependency. There is a real danger, however, of becoming poisoned by bad mushrooms or an unknown substance in the mushrooms. In this case, one needs to call 911 and get to an emergency treatment center as soon as the first signs of trouble develop. Many people have been known to die from bad trips on *Psilocybe* or peyote.

Use of peyote and mushrooms can be psychologically addictive. Dependency on any drug to help one cope with the circumstances of life is not normal.

Some psychologists and anthropolo-

There is no proven danger of physical addiction to magic mushrooms, but there is a real danger of poisoning. If someone has been poisoned by bad mushrooms, call a doctor immediately.

gists believe that the Huichol Indians use peyote daily to keep them from being depressed about their poverty and to deaden the feelings of hunger.

The use of peyote by Native Americans is thought by some to be a way of stepping back into their culture and escaping their problems with the white man's world.

Taking drugs of any kind just to get through a problem is a dangerous habit. If persons are experimenting with mushrooms and peyote, chances are they have tried other drugs. Dependency and addiction may already be established.

A person who has been eating peyote or mushrooms for any length of time should be checked by a physician. Since the chemicals in the plants distort one's senses, a habitual user may suffer from malnutrition. Sometimes people injure themselves during a trip because of the unnatural appearance of size and space.

Seeking Help

Once you know you have a problem, there are many places to go for professional help. The first place is the phone book. Most cities and counties have health services listed in the Government section.

On the inside cover of the phone book you will usually find a list of emergency numbers. Most books have hot lines and 800 numbers to call for drug-related problems. If the number lists a specific drug such as alcohol or cocaine, don't worry about that. The agency will be able to give you information about treatment centers for all major drug-related problems.

Some numbers you can call nationally for information are:

Al-Anon Family Group Headquarters
1-800-356-9996

50

National Clearinghouse for Alcohol
and Drug Information
1-800-729-6686

National Council on Alcoholism and
Drug Dependence Hope Line
1-800-NCA-Call (1-800-622-2255)

Data Center for Drugs and Crime
1-800-666-3332 (These people distrib-
ute a handbook entitled "Drugs,
Crime and the Justice System")

If a family member is in trouble, you
can call the above numbers for help in
coping with the problem. They will give
you the names and numbers of local
agencies to contact. They can also advise
you on methods of intervention.

If a family member has been arrested
in Mexico or another foreign country for
a drug-related crime, you will need to
contact the U.S. State Department and
the American Embassy in the foreign
country. They will be able to tell you
where you can get help.

Support Groups
It is impossible to break dependency and
drug use habits alone. Try to establish a

Our brains judge the size of things by context. When you are hallucinating, your mind may not be able to do this. A set of stairs might look like this to you.

52 | support group, people who will stand by you through those tough moments when you feel the need for a drug.

When seeking help, it is important to involve your family. Addiction and drug use affect the whole family directly or indirectly. Sometimes families are the cause of a dependency. Many teens use drugs to escape abuse, divorcing parents, family arguments and fighting, neglect, or stifling restrictions. If this is so, the problems that cause the drug use need to be resolved before you can think of changing your habits. Try to involve all of the family in the solution and treatment.

Family members are usually the first choice of support, since blood ties are likely to be strong and lasting. Also, members of your family know you well. They know your strengths and your weaknesses. They know when to bolster you up and when to leave you alone.

Friends

Family, however, is not always an available source of help. Friends can be a source, but friendship often is fickle. It is hard to keep friends when you are struggling with problems.

Another disadvantage of friends as a

There are many places to meet new friends.

support group is that they may have been involved in substance abuse along with you. They won't want to face your attempts to break away from drugs; that would mean facing their own dependency.

Often it is necessary to find a new set of friends when trying to break away from substance abuse. It is easier to stay away from drugs if the friends you hang out with are not taking drugs. There are many places to meet new friends. Religious groups, community centers, and organizations such as the YMCA offer programs

54 | for teens. Parks and recreation programs offer activities in most communities.

Support groups from treatment centers are excellent sources of friends because you share the same difficulties. Most big cities have government-supported programs where teens can find counseling, usually free of charge. Some people can afford private centers such as Charter Hospital or private clinics. Wherever you find a center, the friends you meet there will be a valuable source of support and help.

Seeking the Divine

Interest in peyote and mushrooms often is connected to a search for the divine. Because peyote and mushroom users claim to see visions and gods, many are drawn to the plants for that specific purpose.

People basically have a built-in desire to know God. Every known culture on earth, present and past, has developed ways to know God. Therefore it is natural to seek out the divine. Every culture has its religion or way of communing with God. It is best to stay within the framework of your own culture and seek God in the time-established ways.

Trying to search in unknown cultures can bring you strange and frightening experiences. Not only that, you are unprepared to face what you see. For example, a person does not just walk into a Christian church and say, "Okay, I'm here. I want to see the angels and experience the miracles." It takes years of devotion and prayer to come to the point of recognizing and knowing the difference between miracles and deceptions.

It is possible to go to another culture or religion and learn the ways of that culture. Anthropologists live for years with the people they are studying and do come to a partial understanding. They can learn to experience the same things. It is easier, however, to find God within the culture you know.

Just because you are born into a culture doesn't mean you will automatically know its path to God. It takes study, prayer, meditation, and teaching to come to those states. It is tempting to take a shortcut and find God with drugs. That way is not truth.

Trying to deal in other worlds by taking drugs is like trying to go into space and live on the moon by taking a drug and dreaming about it rather than training

Try learning about your own culture's religion before experimenting with another culture's.

and preparing with NASA to do the real thing. Sure, it's quicker to go on an imaginary flight, but it isn't real. To go for real involves intensive devotion and years of sacrifice of time and energy to train and learn procedures. Taking drugs to confront God is a shortcut that could be fatal.

If you truly desire to know God and the spirit world, it will require years of devotion and sacrifice of time and energy to train and learn procedures, but it will be truth that you will find, not dreams and hallucinations.

Overcoming Dependency

It has not been proved that peyote or magic mushrooms are addictive. This does not mean that they are not. It simply means that no studies have been done to prove the matter.

Any time you change the chemical makeup of your body, you risk serious damage. The brain is complicated and works within a balanced system. If you alter the system, it stands to reason that you will change the performance.

Physical addiction is not the only danger. Psychological addiction is a very real danger. This means people take the drug

Self-confidence comes from within, not from drugs.

because they *think* they need it or believe they can't get along without it.

This happens in very subtle ways. Sometimes teens take drugs when their friends do or when they plan to be around their friends. They believe that the drug makes them funnier or more comfortable or more sociable.

In our culture we are told to take a pill to make us feel better. We see our parents or other adults have a drink to relax or feel better. Many teens transfer this indulgence to drugs and believe they need to take them to feel better.

Taking drugs does not help one to feel **59**
better. They do not make one funnier or
more friendly. They make one think one
needs them. This is a false security, a
false answer. If you feel you need drugs
for any of these reasons or you know
someone who does, you or they could be
facing psychological addiction.

Breaking physical and psychological
addiction is very difficult, but not impossible. Help is needed, and it is available.
If you are not addicted now, beware of
the real danger of becoming dependent
on any substance for any reason. There
are other ways to seek answers, solve
problems, and find friends. One can overcome any problem with courage and
strength rather than with drugs. There are
people out there who can help.

Glossary
Explaining New Words

addiction   Compulsive need for habit-forming drugs.

alkaloid   Any chemical containing nitrogen, carbon, hydrogen, and oxygen.

anthropologist   Scientist who studies mankind: cultures, origins, and development.

diversity   The condition of being different or having differences.

divine   Relating to God or a god.

fickle   Not firm or steadfast in character.

hallucination   Experience of something that is not really present.

hallucinogen   Agent that produces hallucinations.

high   Slang term for reaction to hallucinogenic drugs.

indigenous   Born or produced in a particular country; native.

intervention   Coming between in order to stop.

Inquisition Period of history when the Catholic Church persecuted certain persons as being of the devil and therefore to be destroyed.

LSD (lysergic acid diethylamide) Synthetic alkaloid derived from a fungus that grows on rye.

mescaline Compound in peyote that causes hallucinations.

PCP—Phencyclidine, a drug used for its hallucinogenic effects.

psilocin An unstable ingredient found in *Psilocybe*.

Psilocybe Genus of psychoactive mushrooms that contain psilocybin.

psilocybin An acidic phosphoric acid ester.

psychedelic Producing hallucinations or having mind-altering powers.

psychoactive Altering mood or behavior.

psychoactive alkaloids Compounds in the mushrooms that cause hallucinations.

urine Yellowish liquid waste from the kidneys.

For Further Reading

Anderson, Edward F. *Peyote: The Divine Cactus.* Tucson: University of Arizona Press, 1985.

Crow Dog, Mary. *Lakota Woman.* New York: Harper Perennial, 1991.

Furst, Peter T., Ph.D. *Mushrooms, Psychedelic Fungi.* New York: Chelsea House Publishers, 1992.

Hurwitz, Ricki. *Hallucinogens.* New York: Rosen Publishing Group, 1992.

McFarland, Rhoda. *Coping with Substance Abuse,* rev. ed. New York: Rosen Publishing Group, 1990.

Myerhoff Barbara G. *Peyote Hunt, Sacred Journey of the Huichol Indians.* Ithaca: Cornell University Press, 1974.

Newcomb, Michael D., and Bentler, Peter M. *Consequences of Adolescent Drug Use.* Newbury Park: Sage Publications, 1988.

Rawls, Bea O'Donnell. *Drugs and Where to Turn.* New York: Rosen Publishing Group, 1993.

Smith, Sandra Lee. *Coping with Decision-Making,* rev. ed. New York: Rosen Publishing Group, 1993.

Index

About the Author

For twenty-one years, Sandra Lee Smith has taught grades from kindergarten through college level in California and Arizona.

Active on legislative committees and in community projects, she helped design programs to involve parents in the education process.

In response to the President's Report, *A Nation at Risk*, Ms. Smith participated in a project involving Arizona State University, Phoenix Elementary School District, and an inner-city community in Phoenix. Participants in the project developed a holistic approach to education.

Photo Credits

Cover photo: © Maje Waldo
Photos on pages 10, 13, 16, 27 © AP/Wide World Photos; all other photos: © Lauren Piperno